Book 1
Python Programming Professional Made Easy

BY SAM KEY

&

Book 2
Excel Shortcuts

BY SAM KEY

Book 1
Python Programming Professional Made Easy

By Sam Key

Expert Python Programming Language Success in a Day for Any Computer User!

Programming Box Set #44: Python Programming Professional Made Easy & Excel Shortcuts

Table Of Contents

Introduction

I want to thank you and congratulate you for purchasing the book, "Python Programming Professional Made Easy: Expert Python Programming Language Success in a Day for Any Computer User!"

This book contains proven steps and strategies on how to program Python in a few days. The lessons ingrained here will serve as an introduction to the Python language and programming to you. With the little things you will learn here, you will still be able to create big programs.

The book is also designed to prepare you for advanced Python lessons. Make sure that you take note of all the pointers included here since they will help you a lot in the future.

Thanks again for purchasing this book. I hope you enjoy it!

Chapter 1: Introduction to Programming Languages

This short section is dedicated to complete beginners in programming. Knowing all the things included in this chapter will lessen the confusion that you might encounter while learning Python or any programming language.

Computers do not know or cannot do anything by itself. They just appear smart because of the programs installed on them.

Computer, Binary, or Machine Language

You cannot just tell a computer to do something using human language since they can only understand computer language, which is also called machine or binary language. This language only consists of 0's and 1's.

On the other hand, you may not know how to speak or write computer language. Even if you do, it will take you hours before you can tell a computer to do one thing since just one command may consist of hundreds or thousands of 1's and 0's. If you translate one letter in the human alphabet to them, you will get two or three 1's or 0's in return. Just imagine how many 1's and 0's you will need to memorize if you translate a sentence to computer language.

Assembly or Low Level Programming Language

In order to overcome that language barrier, programmers have developed assemblers. Assemblers act as translators between a human and a computer.

However, assemblers cannot comprehend human language. They can only translate binary language to assembly language and vice versa. So, in order to make use of assemblers, programmers need to learn their language, which is also called a low level language.

Unfortunately, assembly language is difficult to learn and memorize. Assembly language consists of words made from mnemonics that only computer experts know. And for one to just make the computer display something to the screen, a programmer needs to type a lot of those words.

High Level Programming Language

Another solution was developed, and that was high level programming languages such as C++, Java, and Python. High level programming languages act as a translator for humans and assembly language or humans to computer language.

Unlike assembly language (or low level language), high level programming languages are easier to understand since they commonly use English words instead of mnemonics. With it, you can also write shorter lines of codes since they already provide commonly used functions that are shortened into one or two keywords.

If you take one command or method in Python and translate it to assembly language, you will have long lines of codes. If you translate it to computer language, you will have thousands of lines composed of 1's and 0's.

In a nutshell, high level programming languages like Python are just translators for humans and computers to understand each other. In order for computers to do something for humans, they need to talk or instruct them via programming languages.

Many high level languages are available today. Among the rest, Python is one of the easiest languages to learn. In the next chapter, you will learn how to speak and write with Python language for your computer to do your bidding.

Chapter 2: Getting Prepped Up

On the previous chapter, you have learned the purpose of programming languages. By choosing this book, you have already decided that Python is the language that you want to use to make your programs. In this chapter, your learning of speaking, writing, and using this language starts.

You, Python, and Your Computer

Before you start writing, take a moment to understand the relationship between you, the programming language, and the computer. Imagine that you are a restaurant manager, and you have hired two foreign guys to cook for the restaurant, which is the program you want to create. The diners in your restaurant are the users of your program.

The first guy is the chef who only knows one language that you do not know. He follows recipes to the letter, and he does not care if the recipe includes him jumping off the cliff. That guy is your computer.

The second guy is the chef's personal translator who will translate the language you speak or write, which is Python, to the language the chef knows. This translator is strict and does not tolerate typos in the recipes he translates. If he finds any mistake, he will tell it right to your face, walk away with the chef, and leave things undone.

He also does not care if the recipe tells the chef to run on circles until he dies. That is how they work. This guy is your programming language.

Since it is a hassle to tell them the recipe while they cook, you decided to write a recipe book instead. That will be your program's code that the translator will read to the chef.

Installing Python

You got two things to get to program in Python. First, get the latest release of Python. Go to this website: https://www.python.org/downloads/.

Download Python 3.4.2 or anything newer than that. Install it. Take note of the directory where you will install Python.

Once you are done with the installation, you must get a source code editor. It is recommended that you get Notepad++. If you already have a source code editor, no need to install Notepad++, too. To download Notepad++, go to: http://www.notepad-plus-plus.org/download/v6.6.9.html. Download and install it.

Version 2.x or 3.x

If you have already visited the Python website to download the program, you might have seen that there are two Python versions that you can download. As of this writing, the first version is Python 3.4.2 and the second version is Python 2.7.8.

About that, it is best that you get the latest version, which is version 3.4.2. The latest version or build will be the only one getting updates and fixes. The 2.7.8 was already declared as the final release for the 2.x build.

Beginners should not worry about it. It is recommended that new Python programmers start with 3.x or later before thinking about exploring the older versions of Python.

Programming and Interactive Mode

Python has two modes. The first one is Programming and the second one is Interactive. You will be using the Interactive mode for the first few chapters of this book. On the other hand, you will be using the Programming mode on the last few chapters.

In Interactive mode, you can play around with Python. You can enter lines of codes on it, and once you press enter, Python will immediately provide a feedback or execute the code you input. To access Python's interactive mode, go to the directory where you installed Python and open the Python application. If you are running on Windows, just open the Run prompt, enter python, and click OK.

In Programming mode, you can test blocks of code in one go. Use a source editor to write the program. Save it as a .py file, and run it as Python program. In Windows, .py files will be automatically associated with Python after you install Python. Due to that, you can just double click the file, and it will run.

Chapter 3: Statements

A program's code is like a recipe book. A book contains chapters, paragraphs, and sentences. On the other hand, a program's code contains modules, functions, and statements. Modules are like chapters that contain the recipes for a full course meal. Procedures or functions are like paragraphs or sections that contain recipes. Statements are like the sentences or steps in a recipe. To code a program with Python, you must learn how to write statements.

Statements

Statements are the building blocks of your program. Each statement in Python contains one instruction that your computer will follow. In comparison to a sentence, statements are like imperative sentences, which are sentences that are used to issue commands or requests. Unlike sentences, Python, or programming languages in general, has a different syntax or structure.

For example, type the statement below on the interpreter:

print("Test")

Press the enter key. The interpreter will move the cursor to the next line and print 'Test' without the single quotes. The command in the sample statement is print. The next part is the details about the command the computer must do. In the example, it is ("test"). If you convert that to English, it is like you are commanding the computer to print the word Test on the program.

Python has many commands and each of them has unique purpose, syntax, and forms. For example, type this and press enter:

1 + 1

Python will return an answer, which is 2. The command there is the operator plus sign. The interpreter understood that you wanted to add the two values and told the computer to send the result of the operation.

Variables

As with any recipe, ingredients should be always present. In programming, there will be times that you would want to save some data in case you want to use them later in your program. And there is when variables come in.

Variables are data containers. They are the containers for your ingredients. You can place almost any type of data on them like numbers or text. You can change the value contained by a variable anytime. And you can use them anytime as long as you need them.

To create one, all you need is to think of a name or identifier for the variable and assign or place a value to it. To create and assign a value to variables, follow the example below:

example1 = 10

On the left is the variable name. On the right is the value you want to assign to the variable. If you just want to create a variable, you can just assign 0 to the variable to act as a placeholder. In the middle is the assignment operator, which is the equal sign. That operator tells the interpreter that you want him to assign a value, which is on its right, to the name or object on the left.

To check if the variable example1 was created and it stored the value 10 in it, type the variable name on the interpreter and press enter. If you done it correctly, the interpreter will reply with the value of the variable. If not, it will reply with a NameError: name <variable_name> is not defined. It means that no variable with that name was created.

Take note, you cannot just create any name for a variable. You need to follow certain rules to avoid receiving syntax errors when creating them. And they are:

- Variable names should start with an underscore or a letter.
- Variable names must only contain letters, numbers, or underscores.
- Variable names can be one letter long or any length.
- Variable names must not be the same with any commands or reserved keywords in Python.
- Variable names are case sensitive. The variable named example1 is different from the variable named Example1.

As a tip, always use meaningful names for your variables. It will help you remember them easily when you are writing long lines of codes. Also, keep them short and use only one style of naming convention. For example, if you create a variable like thisIsAString make sure that you name your second variable like that too: thisIsTheSecondVariable not this_is_the_second_variable.

You can do a lot of things with variables. You can even assign expressions to them. By the way, expressions are combinations of numbers and/or variables together with operators that can be evaluated by the computer. For example:

Example1 = 10

Example2 = 5 + 19

Example3 = Example1 - Example2

If you check the value of those variables in the interpreter, you will get 10 for Example1, 24 for Example2, and -14 for Example3.

Chapter 4: Basic Operators – Part 1

As of this moment, you have already seen three operators: assignment (=), addition (+), and subtraction (-) operators. You can use operators to process and manipulate the data and variables you have – just like how chefs cut, dice, and mix their ingredients.

Types of Python Operators

Multiple types of operators exist in Python. They are:

- **Arithmetic**
- **Assignment**
- **Comparison**
- **Logical**
- **Membership**
- **Identity**
- **Bitwise**

Up to this point, you have witnessed how arithmetic and assignment operators work. During your first few weeks of programming in Python, you will be also using comparison and logical operators aside from arithmetic and assignment operators. You will mostly use membership, identity, and bitwise later when you already advanced your Python programming skills.

As a reference, below is a list of operators under arithmetic and assignment. In the next chapter, comparison and logical will be listed and discussed briefly in preparation for later lessons.

For the examples that the list will use, x will have a value of 13 and y will have a value of 7.

Arithmetic

Arithmetic operators perform mathematical operations on numbers and variables that have numbers stored on them.

> + : Addition. Adds the values besides the operator.

z = 13 + 7

z's value is equal to 20.

- : Subtraction. Subtracts the values besides the operator.

z = x – y

z's value is equal to 6.

* : **Multiplication. Multiplies the values besides the operator.**

z = x * y

z's value is equal to 91.

/ : **Division. Divides the values besides the operator.**

z = x / y

z's value is equal to 1.8571428571428572.

** : **Exponent. Applies exponential power to the value to the left (base) with the value to the right (exponent).**

z = x ** y

z's value is equal to 62748517.

// : **Floor Division. Divides the values besides the operator and returns a quotient with removed digits after the decimal point.**

z = x // y

z's value is equal to 1.

% : **Modulus. Divides the values besides the operator and returns the remainder instead of the quotient.**

z = x % y

z's value is equal to 6.

Assignment

Aside from the equal sign or simple assignment operator, other assignment operators exist. Mostly, they are combinations of arithmetic operators and the simple assignment operator.

They are used as shorthand methods when reassigning a value to a variable that is also included in the expression that will be assigned to it. Using them in your code simplifies and makes your statements clean.

= : **Simple assignment operator. It assigns the value of the expression on its right hand side to the variable to its left hand side.**

z = x + y * x – y % x

z's value is equal to 97.

The following assignment operators work like this: it applies the operation first on the value of the variable on its left and the result of the expression on its right. After that, it assigns the result of the operation to the variable on its left.

+= : Add and Assign

x += y

x's value is equal to 20. It is equivalent to x = x + y.

-= : Subtract and Assign

x −= y

x's value is equal to 6. It is equivalent to x = x – y.

*= : Multiply and assign

x *= y

x's value is equal to 91. It is equivalent to x = x * y.

/= : Divide and assign

x /= y

x's value is equal to 1.8571428571428572. It is equivalent to x = x / y.

**= : Exponent and Assign

x **= y

x's value is equal to 62748517. It is equivalent to x = x ** y.

//= : Floor Division and Assign

x //= y

x's value is equal to 1. It is equivalent to x = x // y.

%= : Modulus and Assign

x %= y

x's value is equal to 6. It is equivalent to x = x % y.

Multiple Usage of Some Operators

Also, some operators may behave differently depending on how you use them or what values you use together with them. For example:

z = “sample” + “statement”

As you can see, the statement tried to add two strings. In other programming languages, that kind of statement will return an error since their (+) operator is dedicated for addition of numbers only. In Python, it will perform string concatenation that will append the second string to the first. Hence, the value of variable z will become “samplestatement”.

On the other hand, you can use the (-) subtraction operator as unary operators. To denote that a variable or number is negative, you can place the subtraction operator before it. For example:

z = 1 - -1

The result will be 2 since 1 minus negative 1 is 2.

The addition operator acts as a unary operator for other languages; however, it behaves differently in Python. In some language, an expression like this: +(-1), will be treated as positive 1. In Python, it will be treated as +1(-1), and if you evaluate that, you will still get negative 1.

To perform a unary positive, you can do this instead:

--1

In that example, Python will read it as –(-1) or -1 * -1 and it will return a positive 1.

Chapter 5: Basic Operators – Part 2

Operators seem to be such a big topic, right? You will be working with them all the time when programming in Python. Once you master or just memorize them all, your overall programming skills will improve since most programming languages have operators that work just like the ones in Python.

And just like a restaurant manager, you would not want to let your chef serve food with only unprocessed ingredients all the time. Not everybody wants salads for their dinner.

Comparison

Aside from performing arithmetic operations and storing values to variables, Python can also allow you to let the computer compare expressions. For example, you can ask your computer if 10 is greater than 20. Since 10 is greater than 20, it will reply with True – meaning the statement you said was correct. If you have compared 20 is greater than 10 instead, it will return a reply that says False.

== : Is Equal

z = x == y

z's value is equal to FALSE.

!= : Is Not Equal

z = x != y

z's value is equal to True.

> : Is Greater Than

z = x > y

z's value is equal to True.

< : Is Less Than

z = x < y

z's value is equal to FALSE.

>= : Is Greater Than or Equal

z = x >= y

z's value is equal to True.

<= : Is Less Than or Equal

z = x <= y

z's value is equal to FALSE.

Note that the last two operators are unlike the combined arithmetic and simple assignment operator.

Logical

Aside from arithmetic and comparison operations, the computer is capable of logical operations, too. Even simple circuitry can do that, but that is another story to tell.

Anyway, do you remember your logic class where your professor talked about truth tables, premises, and propositions? Your computer can understand all of that. Below are the operators you can use to perform logic in Python. In the examples in the list, a is equal to True and b is equal to False.

and : Logical Conjunction AND. It will return only True both the propositions or variable besides it is True. It will return False if any or both the propositions are False.

w = a and a

x = a and b

y = b and a

z = b and b

w is equal to True, x is equal to False, y is equal to False, and z is equal to False.

or : Logical Disjunction OR. It will return True if any or both of the proposition or variable beside it is True. It will return False if both the propositions are False.

w = a or a

x = a or b

y = b or a

z = b or b

w is equal to True, x is equal to True, y is equal to True, and z is equal to False.

not : Logical Negation NOT. Any Truth value besides it will be negated. If True is negated, the computer will reply with a False. If False is negated, the computer will reply with a True.

w = not a

x = not b

w is equal to False and x is equal to True.

If you want to perform Logical NAND, you can use Logic Negation NOT and Logical Conjunction AND. For example:

w = not (a and a)

x = not (a and b)

y = not (b and a)

z = not (b and b)

w is equal to False, x is equal to True, y is equal to True, and z is equal to True.

If you want to perform Logical NOR, you can use Logic Negation NOT and Logical Disjunction OR. For example:

w = not (a or a)

x = not (a or b)

y = not (b or a)

z = not (b or b)

w is equal to False, x is equal to False, y is equal to False, and z is equal to True.

You can perform other logical operations that do not have Python operators by using conditional statements, which will be discussed later in this book.

Order of Precedence

In case that your statement contains multiple types or instances of operators, Python will evaluate it according to precedence of the operators, which is similar to the PEMDAS rule in Mathematics. It will evaluate the operators with the highest precedence to the lowest. For example:

z = 2 + 10 / 10

Instead of adding 2 and 10 first then dividing the sum by 10, Python will divide 10 by 10 first then add 2 to the quotient instead since division has a higher precedence than subtraction. So, instead of getting 1.2, you will get 3.0. In case that it confuses you, imagine that Python secretly adds parentheses to the expression. The sample above is the same as:

z = 2 + (10 / 10)

If two operators with the same level of precedence exist in one statement, Python will evaluate the first operator that appears from the left. For example:

z = 10 / 10 * 2

The value of variable z will be 2.

Take note that any expressions inside parentheses or nested deeper in parentheses will have higher precedence than those expressions outside the parentheses. For example:

z = 2 / ((1 + 1) * (2 – 4))

Even though the division operator came first and has higher precedence than addition and subtraction, Python evaluated the ones inside the parentheses first and evaluated the division operation last. So, it added 1 and 1, subtracted 4 from 2, multiplied the sum and difference of the two previous operations, and then divided the product from 2. The value of variable z became -0.5.

Below is a reference for the precedence of the operations. The list is sorted from operations with high precedence to operators with low precedence.

- **Exponents**
- **Unary**
- **Multiplication, Division, Modulo, and Floor Division**
- **Addition, and Subtraction**
- **Bitwise**
- **Comparison**
- **Assignment**
- **Identity**
- **Membership**
- **Logical**

Truth Values

The values True and False are called truth values – or sometimes called Boolean data values. The value True is equal to 1 and the value False is equal to 0. That means that you can treat or use 1 as the truth value True and 0 as the truth value False. Try comparing those two values in your interpreter. Code the following:

True == 1

False == 0

The interpreter will return a value of True – meaning, you can interchange them in case a situation arises. However, it is advisable that that you use them like that sparingly.

Another thing you should remember is that the value True and False are case sensitive. True != TRUE or False != false. Aside from that, True and False are Python keywords. You cannot create variables named after them.

You might be wondering about the use of truth values in programming. The answer is, you can use them to control your programs using conditional or flow control tools. With them, you can make your program execute statements when a certain condition arises. And that will be discussed on the next chapter.

Chapter 6: Functions, Flow Control, and User Input

With statements, you have learned to tell instructions to the computer using Pythons. As of now, all you know is how to assign variables and manipulate expressions. And the only command you know is print. Do you think you can make a decent program with those alone? Maybe, but you do not need to rack your brains thinking of one.

In this chapter, you will learn about functions and flow control. This time, you will need to leave the interpreter or Interactive mode. Open your source code editor since you will be programming blocks of codes during this section.

Functions

Statements are like sentences in a book or steps in a recipe. On the other hand, functions are like paragraphs or a recipe in a recipe book. Functions are blocks of code with multiple statements that will perform a specific goal or goals when executed. Below is an example:

```
def recipe1():

        print("Fried Fish Recipe")

        print("Ingredients:")

        print("Fish")

        print("Salt")

        print("Steps:")

        print("1. Rub salt on fish.")

        print("2. Fry fish.")

        print("3. Serve.")
```

The function's purpose is to print the recipe for Fried Fish. To create a function, you will need to type the keyword def (for define) then the name of the function. In the example, the name of the function is recipe1. The parentheses are important to be present there. It has its purpose, but for now, leave it alone.

After the parentheses, a colon was placed. The colon signifies that a code block will be under the function.

To include statements inside that code block, you must indent it. In the example, one indentation or tab was used. To prevent encountering errors, make sure that all the statements are aligned and have the same number of indentations.

To end the code block for the function, all you need is to type a statement that has the same indentation level of the function declaration.

By the way, all the statements inside a function code block will not be executed until the function is called or invoked. To invoke the function, all you need is to call it using its name. To invoke the function recipe1, type this:

recipe1()

And that is how simple functions work.

Flow Control

It is sad that only one recipe can be displayed by the sample function. It would be great if your program can display more recipes. And letting the user choose the recipe that they want to be displayed on the program would be cool. But how can you do that?

You can do that by using flow control tools in Python. With them, you can direct your program to do something if certain conditions are met. In the case of the recipe listing program, you can apply flow control and let them see the recipes by requesting it.

If Statement

The simplest control flow tool you can use for this type of project is the if statement. Have you been wondering about truth values? Now, you can use them with if statements.

An *if statement* is like a program roadblock. If the current condition of your program satisfies its requirements, then it will let it access the block of statements within it. It is like a function with no names, and instead of being invoked to work, it needs you to satisfy the conditions set to it. For example:

```
a = 2

if a == 2:

        print("You satisfied the condition!")

        print("This is another statement that will be executed!")

if a == (1 + 1):

        print("You satisfied the condition again!")

        print("I will display the recipe for Fried Fish!")

        recipe1()
```

If you will translate the first if statement in English, it will mean that: if variable a is equals to 2, then print the sentence inside the parentheses. Another way to translate it is: if the comparison between variable a and the number 2 returns True, then print the sentence inside the parentheses.

As you can see, the colon is there and the statements below the if statement are indented, too. It really is like a function.

User Input

You can now control the flow of your program and create functions. Now, about the recipe program, how can the user choose the recipe he wants to view? That can be done by using the input() command. You can use it like this:

a = input("Type your choice here and press enter: ")

Once Python executes that line, it will stop executing statements. And provide a prompt that says "Type your choice here: ". During that moment, the user will be given a chance to type something in the program. If the user press enter, Python will store and assign the characters the user typed on the program to variable a. Once that process is done, Python will resume executing the statements after the input statement.

In some cases, programmers use the input command to pause the program and wait for the user to press enter. You can do that by just placing input() on a line.

With that, you can make a program that can capture user input and can change its flow whenever it gets the right values from the user. You can create a recipe program that allows users to choose the recipe they want. Here is the code. Analyze it. And use the things you have learned to improve it. Good luck.

```
print("Enter the number of the recipe you want to read.")

print("1 - Fried Fish")

print("2 - Fried Egg")

print("Enter any character to Exit")

choice = input("Type a Number and Press Enter: ")


if choice == "1":

    print("Fried Fish Recipe")

    print("Ingredients:")

    print("Fish")
```

```
    print("Salt")
    print("Steps:")
    print("1. Rub salt on fish.")
    print("2. Fry fish.")
    print("3. Serve.")
    pause = input("Press enter when you are done reading.")

if choice == "2":
    print("Fried Egg Recipe")
    print("Ingredients:")
    print("Egg")
    print("Salt")
    print("Steps:")
    print("1. Fry egg.")
    print("2. Sprinkle Salt.")
    print("3. Serve.")
    pause = input("Press enter when you are done reading.")
```

Conclusion

Thank you again for purchasing this book!

I hope this book was able to help you to learn the basics of Python programming.

The next step is to learn more about Python! You should have expected that coming.

Kidding aside, with the current knowledge you have in Python programming, you can make any programs like that with ease. But of course, there are still lots of things you need to learn about the language such as loops, classes, and etcetera.

Finally, if you enjoyed this book, please take the time to share your thoughts and post a review on Amazon. We do our best to reach out to readers and provide the best value we can. Your positive review will help us achieve that. It'd be greatly appreciated!

Thank you and good luck!

Book 2
Excel Shortcuts

By Sam Key

The 100 Top Best Powerful Excel Keyboard Shortcuts in 1 Day!

Table Of Contents

Introduction

I want to thank you and congratulate you for purchasing the book, "The Power of Excel Shortcuts: The 100 Top Best Powerful Excel Keyboard Shortcuts in 1 Day!".

This book contains proven steps and strategies on how to master the Microsoft Excel through just 100 keyboard shortcuts! However, most people will ask, "Why do you need to learn these shortcuts anyway?"

Advantages of Using Microsoft Excel

Microsoft Excel has become one of the most commonly used enterprise software in schools and offices. Its way of presenting data, which is through a spreadsheet, has helped a lot of people especially in the field of data mining. If you were going to put numerous rows of data, in let's say, a word processing program, it might take a lot of time creating tables and formatting each of them to fit in the pages. With the Microsoft Excel, these manual tasks are now much easier.

What does the Microsoft Excel have that other programs don't? For one, it has a built-in spreadsheet that you can manipulate the size and formatting. This versatile way of maneuvering the spreadsheet made it indispensable for many. Now, gone are the days were people have to manually draw tables in sheets of paper. Excel has already the tables prepared for them.

Another nifty feature of this software is its calculation function. Excel houses a myriad of formulas for solving arithmetic, financial and logical problems, among others. Thus, one doesn't even need to calculate every sum or average of a data series. Just by using a formula in Excel, everything can be done in an instant.

The Secret behind Mastering Excel

Speaking of instant, did you know that Excel has more than a hundred keyboard shortcuts? What does this mean to you as an Excel user? It means you can continuously work on your Excel spreadsheet without having to depend on your mouse constantly for Excel functions.

This is especially helpful whenever you are inputting a lot of data, and doing this will be more efficient if both of your hands weren't switching from keyboard to mouse and vice versa, every once in a while. In addition, if your mouse suddenly chose the most inopportune time to malfunction, learning Excel shortcuts can save you from major headaches.

As such, this book will provide you 100 keyboard shortcuts which you can use in Excel. In addition, as a bonus, you will learn about alternatives in case you forget any of these shortcuts.

Thanks again for purchasing this book, I hope you enjoy it!

Chapter 1: Moving Around the Excel Screen

People typically use the mouse for navigating the Excel screen. With this device, you can manipulate every cell in Excel, including its formatting and color. Since the mouse can access the major functions in Excel through the ribbon, there is no need for you to manually-type every formula or command.

However, the only difficult thing that you cannot do with a mouse is entering text. If you're going to use an on-screen keyboard, keying in the data in every cell would probably take you a lot longer than just using the keyboard for the text.

Thus, if you're going to use the keyboard most of the time, especially if you're just starting to build the spreadsheet data from scratch, it would be helpful to learn the basic keyboard shortcuts for moving around the Excel spreadsheet.

Shortcut #1: Arrow Keys

There are four arrow keys found in the right side of your main keyboard keys. These are the Arrow Left, Arrow Right, Arrow Up, and Arrow Down keys. Intuitively, you know that you can use these keys for moving within the spreadsheet. For instance, by selecting a cell then pressing Arrow Up, it will situate the cursor in the cell directly above your selected cell.

Shortcut #2: Ctrl + Arrow Key

Let's assume that you have a block of Excel data that spans more than 50,000 rows and more than 200 columns. You would probably have a hard time using a mouse in skimming these voluminous data. As such, you can use the Ctrl + Arrow key to navigate each "ends" of the data easily. In this example, click any cell in the block of data then press Ctrl + Arrow Down. You will be immediately located to the bottom cell in that specific column.

Shortcut #3: Shift + Arrow Key

You have selected all the items in the row but you forgot to include one cell. What would you do if you needed to include the next cell in the selection? Simply press Shift + Arrow Key, where the arrow pertains to the direction of the region you want to highlight.

Shortcut #4: Ctrl + Shift + Arrow Key

The above shortcut only includes one cell in the selection; but what would happen if you want to include everything until the last cell containing a data? You then use the Ctrl + Shift + Arrow Key.

Shortcut #5: Backspace

The Backspace key immediately deletes the contents of the active cell. However, if the cell is in Edit mode, it will only delete one character in the left of the insertion point, or the blinking cursor in the Formula bar.

Shortcut #6: Delete

This key has the same function as the Backspace key. However, instead of the left side, it removes a character in the right hand side of the insertion point.

Shortcut #7: End

Pressing the End key will enable the End Mode in Excel. In this mode, if you press an Arrow key, it will directly take you to the last used cell (or if none, last cell) in that specific direction. However, if the Scroll Lock is on, pressing the End key will only take you to the lower right corner of your Excel screen.

Shortcut #8: Ctrl + End

It works the same as the End key where pressing this combination will take you to the last used cell. However, if no cells were used, it will not move to the end of the worksheet like the End key does. Also, if the insertion point is located in the Formula bar (e.g., after the first character), Ctrl + End will put this cursor at the end of the field.

Shortcut #9: Ctrl + Shift + End

This keyboard shortcut can do two functions. First, in the Formula bar, it will select every character at the right of the insertion point. On the other hand, if you use it in the worksheet, it will highlight the cells starting from the active cell (or selected cell) until the last used cell in the worksheet.

Shortcut #10: Spacebar

Aside from putting a space in your text, it can also either select or clear a checkbox.

Shortcut #11: Ctrl + Spacebar

This will select the whole column to where the active cell is located.

Shortcut #12: Shift + Spacebar

It has the same function as the above, but this shortcut selects rows instead of columns.

Shortcut #13: Ctrl + Shift + Spacebar

Pressing these keys will select your entire worksheet.

Shortcut #14: Enter

After you have entered a data in a cell, pressing the Enter key will complete the input of data. Besides that, you can also directly go one cell below through this key. Considered as the most commonly used shortcut in Excel, you will be using the Enter key quite a lot because all Excel functions need it.

Shortcut #15: Shift + Enter

If you press Enter, you will go down one cell. Conversely, a Shift + Enter will complete an entry in a cell but the cursor will go directly above your entry.

Shortcut #16: Ctrl + Enter

Since this is a spreadsheet, it follows that after you have put an entry, you will enter another data below it. That is the common task whenever you're working on a table or database, which explains why the Enter key goes down. However, if you think that you need the downward movement, you can try Ctrl + Enter. This will plainly enter your data in the cell and it won't move your cursor to another direction.

Shortcut #17: Alt + Enter

You want the data to go into the next line in the same cell. However, if you press Enter, the cursor just moves on to the next cell in line. Pressing the Tab key doesn't work either. So what will you do? Try Alt + Enter key and see if it works.

Shortcut #18: Esc Key

The Escape key, or simply "Esc", performs a lot of nifty functions in Excel. Among of which are the following: 1) deletes a whole data in a cell, 2) exits you from a dialog box, and 3) escapes you from the full screen mode of Excel.

Shortcut #19: Home Key

The Home key will take you to the first cell in the specific row of your active cell. However, if the Scroll Lock is on, the cursor will go to the upper-left corner of your current window.

Shortcut #20: Ctrl + Home

This shortcut, also known as the "True Home key", brings the user to the beginning of the worksheet.

Shortcut #21: Ctrl + Shift + Home

This will select all cells from the active cell up to the first cell in the worksheet.

Shortcut #22: Page Down

Scouring among rows and rows of worksheets is now easy because of this button. This will display the next page in your Excel window.

Shortcut #23: Alt + Page Down

Unlike Page Down, the Alt + Page Down combination will show the next page to the right of your current window.

Shortcut #24: Ctrl + Page Down

Flipping in several worksheets is now easy thanks to Ctrl + Page Down. This will automatically turn you over to the next worksheet.

Shortcut #25: Ctrl + Shift + Page Down

The normal way of selecting several worksheets at once is to hold Ctrl while clicking each of the worksheets to be included in the selection. However, for those who don't think this is the practical way to do it, here's an alternative. Use the Ctrl + Shift + Page Down; it will automatically select the sheets for you.

Shortcut #26: Page Up

This is quite similar to Shortcut #22: Page Down key, except for the fact that this one goes in the opposite direction (which is upward).

Shortcut #27: Alt + Page Up

The Alt + Page Up will move your screen to the left, instead of right as what was described in Shortcut #23: Alt + Page Down.

Shortcut #28: Ctrl + Page Up

Same as Shortcut #24: Ctrl + Page Down, this will enable you to change sheets easily. However, this one goes in a counterclockwise direction.

Shortcut #29: Ctrl + Shift + Page Up

Selecting sheets is also a function of the Ctrl + Shift + Page Up. However, it will select the worksheets on the left hand side of your current sheet first.

Shortcut #30: Tab Key

Using the Tab key will enable you to move to the right hand side of the cell. Also, if you have a protected worksheet, pressing this can immediately take you to the next unlocked cell. Lastly, in case there is a dialog box, you can easily move along the options through the Tab key.

Shortcut #31: Shift + Tab

The Shift + Tab works the opposite way; if pressing Tab will take you to the right hand cell, this shortcut will locate the left cell for you. It also applies to the other functions of the Tab key. In a dialog box for instance, keying in Shift + Tab will move you to the previous option.

Shortcut #32: Ctrl + Tab

You're now done with shortcuts for moving around cells and worksheets. As such, the succeeding shortcuts in this chapter will focus on dialog boxes. For this shortcut, use it if you want to go to the next tab in a dialog box.

Shortcut #33: Ctrl + Shift + Tab

However, if you wish to go back to the previous tab in a dialog box, using the Ctrl + Shift + Tab is the right combination.

So there you have it, the first 33 keyboard shortcuts in Excel. Hopefully, through these tips you can know traverse in your multitude of cells and worksheets with no difficulty at all.

Chapter 2: Navigating the Excel Ribbon

Microsoft created the "ribbon" as a replacement to the expanding menus in the earlier versions of Microsoft Excel. It houses all the functions in Excel such as formatting, page layout, pictures, and shapes. However, since its interface is not in an expanding menu style, people are not that familiar with its keyboard shortcuts as compared to before where you can immediately see which shortcut runs which.

To help you with that, here are some of the most commonly used keyboard shortcuts for exploring the Ribbon.

Shortcut #34: Alt Key

Letters and numbers will appear in the ribbon once you push the Alt key. What happens is that it activates the access keys, wherein typing in corresponding letter or number will let you select a specific function in the ribbon.

Shortcut #35: F10

This key has the same function as the Alt key, only that pressing the F10 would require you to use your right hand instead.

Shortcut #36: Alt + Arrow Left/Right

To be able to navigate to the other tabs, use these keys.

Shortcut #37: F10 + Arrow Left/Right

Since it was previously mentioned that the F10 behaves the same way as the Alt key, pressing F10 followed by an arrow to the left or to the right will also transfer you to other tabs.

Shortcut #38: Ctrl + F1

There's no doubt that the ribbon indeed takes up quite a lot of space in your screen. Therefore, for those who want more area for their spreadsheet, hiding the ribbon is the best option. To do that, simply press Ctrl + F1. To show the ribbon again, also press the same shortcut.

Shortcut #39: Shift + F10

Shift + F10 is similar to the right click button of your mouse. It can open menus and other options depending on where your cursor is.

Shortcut #40: F6

You can move along three areas of the screen through this key. The F6 key, will take you either to the ribbon, the spreadsheet, or the status bar.

Shortcut #41: F10 + Tab

In a tab, you can browse through the functions by pressing this combination continuously. You can also press this shortcut first, and then proceed with the arrow keys for navigation.

Shortcut #42: F10 + Shift + Tab

The above shortcut goes around the functions in a clockwise manner. On the contrary, the F10 + Shift + Tab shortcut does otherwise.

Shortcut #43: F1

In the upper right corner of the ribbon, there is a blue question mark icon. Accessing this icon will take you to the Microsoft Excel Help task pane. Alternatively, if you press F1 the same pane will open.

Since the area around the ribbon is limited, it is only appropriate that there would be less keyboard shortcuts dedicated for it. All in all, there are ten button combinations for the ribbon.

Chapter 3: Formatting the Excel Spreadsheet

If you're also a user of the Microsoft Word, you are probably familiar with formatting keyboard shortcuts such as Ctrl + B, which stands for bold text or Ctrl + I, which italicizes your text. Since you can do almost every basic feature that you need in the Word application through the keyboard, this makes the formatting easier for you.

Fortunately, even though Excel is not a word-processing program, it also has dedicated keyboard shortcuts that for formatting. These are as follows:

Shortcut #44: Alt + ‘

By going to the Styles group in the Home tab, you can quickly change the appearance of the cell by selecting any of the pre-installed styles in Excel. To see the formatting changes done within a cell, you click on the New Style option, which will take you to the Style dialog box. Similarly, clicking Alt + ‘ will get you in the same menu.

Shortcut #45: Ctrl + B

Like in Microsoft Word, Ctrl + B will either apply or remove a bold format in a text.

Shortcut #46: Ctrl + 2

This shortcut can also make the selected text into a bold type.

Shortcut #47: Ctrl + I

Letter I stands for Italics. As such, clicking Ctrl + I will turn any text into an italicized type.

Shortcut #48: Ctrl + 3

This also functions like the Ctrl + I shortcut.

Shortcut #49: Ctrl + U

Ctrl + U will put an underline in the selected text.

Shortcut #50: Ctrl + 4

Another alternative for the Ctrl +U is the Ctrl + 4 shortcut.

Shortcut #51: Ctrl + 5

To easily put a strikethrough in your text, press Ctrl + 5.

Shortcut #52: Ctrl + Shift + F

If you want more font formatting options, you can just proceed to the Font tab of the Format cells dialog box. Right-clicking a cell then selecting Format Cells will get you there, or you can just use this shortcut.

Shortcut #53: Ctrl + Shift + P

This shortcut works the same as the above.

Shortcut #54: Ctrl + Shift + &

Now that you're done with editing the text, this shortcut as well as the succeeding ones will pertain to cell formatting. As for Ctrl + Shift + &, it will put a plain black border on all sides of the cell.

Shortcut #55: Ctrl + Shift + _

On the contrary, Ctrl + Shift + _ will remove the borders that you have made.

Shortcut #56: F4

Instead of manually doing all the formatting for a number of cells, Excel has a shortcut wherein you can redo the formatting that you just did in another cell. This is the F4 function key. For example, if you have put borders in Cell A1, selecting Cell A2 then pressing F4 will also create borders for that specific cell.

Shortcut #57: Ctrl + 1

Pressing the Ctrl + 1 will show the Format Cells dialog box. In this box, you can edit every possible formatting for a cell such as number format, alignment, font, border, and fill.

The previous chapters have discussed how certain shortcuts can perform specific functions in Excel such as formatting cells and navigating the spreadsheet. In the following chapters, the topics will be about the different uses of specific buttons such as the Function keys and the Control key.

Chapter 4: Working with Function Keys

The first row of keys in your keyboard contains the function keys, which is denoted by the letter F followed by a number. In the Windows desktop, these function keys can do a variety of tasks such as adjusting the screen brightness or minimizing the volume.

Excel uses the function keys for different purposes. Thus, most people usually have a difficulty mastering the Function key shortcuts in Excel.

Shortcut #58: Alt + F1

Alt + F1 will automatically create a chart for you. Just select the range of cells containing your chart data then press this shortcut. Afterwards, a column chart will appear in the worksheet.

Shortcut #59: Alt + Shift + F1

The normal way in creating a new worksheet is by right-clicking any of the existing worksheets then choosing Insert. The same task can be done by this shortcut.

Shortcut #60: F2

In editing a formula, you can't just simply select an active cell; you have to click on the Formula bar so that you can make changes to it. Fortunately, the F2 will put the cell in Edit mode. Thus, if you want to amend a cell, there's no need for you to click on the Formula bar; just use F2 instead.

Shortcut #61: Shift + F2

The Shift + F2 shortcut will insert comments in the active cell.

Shortcut #62: Ctrl + F2

Unlike the previous F2 combinations, this one has nothing to do with editing a cell. When you press Ctrl + F2, you will be forwarded to the Print Preview screen. Upon exiting this screen, your spreadsheet will show dotted lines which serves as a marker for a page border.

Shortcut #63: F3

Instead of constantly referring to a range of cells by their cell location (e.g., A1:D1), you can just define a name for this range. Thus, whenever you want to pertain to that specific range in a formula, you can simply put its name; there's no need for you to put the cell range. F3 will take you to the Paste Name dialog box, wherein you can list all the names created in a worksheet and their respective cell references.

Shortcut #64: Ctrl + F3

To create a new name, go to the Name Manager through Ctrl + F3.

Shortcut #65: Shift + F3

Using formulas is the heart of Microsoft Excel. Without it, you cannot do any calculations in the spreadsheet. As such, there is a dedicated tab for Formulas in the Excel ribbon. However, it may take quite a lot of time for users to efficiently look for the appropriate formula with all the possible options in the Formulas tab. Because of this, the Shift + F3 key combination is made. It opens the Insert Function dialog box, wherein you can easily search for a formula by just typing in the description of what you need to do.

Shortcut #66: Ctrl + F4

You don't need to click that "X" mark in the upper left corner of your Excel screen just to close the application; a simple Ctrl + F4 is enough to do the job.

Shortcut #67: F5

Rummaging through a lot of cells takes a lot of work, especially if you're dealing with thousands of rows in a spreadsheet. The Go To dialog box, which can be accessed through F5, will help you reach that specific cell or range that you wanted to see.

Shortcut #68: Ctrl + F5

By default, all workbooks are always in full screen mode in Excel. However, if you're doing work on several Excel files at once, it may be hard to switch from one file to the other when each workbook is on full screen. Through Ctrl + F5, the selected file restore to window size in the Excel screen so that you can easily switch across files.

Shortcut #69: Shift + F6

This works the same as Shortcut #40: F6, albeit in a counterclockwise direction.

Shortcut #70: Ctrl + F6

If you have more than one workbook open, pressing Ctrl + F6 will let you switch among these workbooks.

Shortcut #71: F7

Aside from Microsoft Word, the Excel application has also a built-in spell checker. To check the spelling of every word in your spreadsheet, press F7. This will run the Spelling dialog box. Apart from detecting erroneous spellings, it also suggests possible words that can replace the incorrect word.

Shortcut #72: Ctrl + F7

As mentioned before, you should not use the full screen mode when working with several Excel files. This is so that you can select each workbook with ease. The Ctrl + F7 shortcut executes the Move command so that you can drag the unneeded workbooks in another area in the Excel screen where it can't obstruct your view.

Shortcut #73: F8

Upon pressing F8, the Excel goes into an Extend Selection mode. This enables you to use the arrow keys to extend the current selection. Pressing the same key will also lift the Extend Selection mode.

Shortcut #74: Shift + F8

The limitation of the F8 key is that it only adds adjacent cells in the selection. Through Shift + F8, you can now add any nonadjacent cell by using arrow keys.

Shortcut #75: Ctrl + F8

To resize your workbook, use Ctrl + F8. This will run the Size command for workbooks that are not in a full screen mode.

Shortcut #76: Alt + F8

A macro is a set of actions created using the Visual Basic programming language. What it does is to automate a set of tasks in Excel. For example, you're going to retrieve a data in a one sheet then you'll paste the said data in another sheet. However, if you're going to do the copy-paste task for thousands of data, it might take you a long time. As such, you can use the macro for this. Alt + F8 will open the Macro dialog box, where you can record and run a macro.

Shortcut #77: F9

This is the Refresh button in Excel. Once you refresh a workbook, it will recalculate all new formulas in the said file.

Shortcut #78: Shift + F9

On the other hand, Shift + F9 will only recalculate the formulas in the worksheet you are currently working on.

Shortcut #79: Ctrl + Alt + F9

This has the same function as F9, but it will also recalculate formulas that have not been changed.

Shortcut #80: Ctrl + Alt + Shift + F9

Aside from doing what the Ctrl + Alt + F9 shortcut does, it also rechecks all dependent formulas for any errors.

Shortcut #81: Alt + Shift + F10

Smart tags are data that are labeled in a particular type. For instance, a person's name in an Outlook email message can be labeled with this tag. You can open the smart tag menu through this shortcut.

Shortcut #82: Ctrl + F10

This will enable a workbook to display in full screen mode (or maximized mode).

Shortcut #83: F11

The Shortcut #58: Alt + F1 will let you create charts by highlighting the data series. Similarly, the F11 key has the same function except that you don't need to select the data series; it will automatically detect the data for you. Another difference between these two shortcuts is that the Alt + F1 will display the chart in the same worksheet, while the F1 key will make another worksheet for the new chart.

Shortcut #84: Shift + F11

This is an alternative to Shortcut #59: Alt + Shift + F1, wherein it will insert a new worksheet.

Shortcut #85: Alt + F11

Alt + F11 will open the Microsoft Visual Basic Editor. In this menu, you can create or edit a macro by using the Visual Basic for Applications (VBA) programming language.

Shortcut #86: F12

The F12 key is the shortcut for the Save As dialog box. It lets you save your Excel file among the available formats.

In case you're wondering why the F1, F4, F6 and F10 keys as well as some of their derivatives are not included in the list, these function keys have already been discussed in the previous chapters. Moreover, as this book specifically claims that it will contain at least a hundred keyboard shortcuts, putting these function keys again in the list will not create an accurate count of all the shortcuts.

Chapter 5: Discovering Ctrl Combinations

There are more than 50 Ctrl key combinations that you can use in the Excel sheet, with some shortcuts comprising of special characters instead of the usual alphanumeric ones. Thus, it would be unpractical to include every possible shortcut, especially if there's a little chance that a typical user will use them all.

With these reasons, only the f14 most valuable Ctrl shortcuts will be contained in the list below.

Shortcut #87: Ctrl + ;

Ctrl + ; will show the current date in the active cell.

Shortcut #88: Ctrl + Shift + #

Ctrl + Shift + # will change the date into a day-month-year format.

Shortcut #89: Ctrl + A

This is an alternative to Shortcut #13: Ctrl + Shift + Spacebar. Pressing these keys will also select the whole worksheet.

Shortcut #90: Ctrl + C

Ctrl + C will copy the contents of the active cell.

Shortcut #91: Ctrl + F

If you need to search for a specific data, you don't have to go to the Home tab and choose Find & Select. By pressing Ctrl + F, you can now access the Find and Replace dialog box immediately.

Shortcut #92: Ctrl + K

To insert or edit a hyperlink, use this shortcut.

Shortcut #93: Ctrl + R

This activates the Fill Right command. To use this, simply click on a cell you want filled then press Ctrl + R. It will copy all the formatting and contents of the cell to its left.

Shortcut #94: Ctrl + S

Ctrl + S will automatically save your file in its current name, location and format.

Shortcut #95: Ctrl + V

After doing Shortcut #90: Ctrl + C, you then proceed with Ctrl + V to paste the contents that you have copied.

Shortcut #96: Ctrl + Alt + V

Since the above shortcut will paste all the data as is, the Ctrl + Alt + V will give you most pasting options as it will open the Paste Special dialog box.

Shortcut #97: Ctrl + W

This combination is an alternative to Shortcut #66: Ctrl + F4, which closes the Excel program.

Shortcut #98: Ctrl + X

This will cut the contents of an active cell. When you say “cut”, it will remove the data in a cell and will place it temporarily in the Clipboard so that you can paste the contents in another cell.

Shortcut #99: Ctrl + Y

The Ctrl + Y shortcut runs the Redo function, which means that it will repeat the previous command that you have done.

Shortcut #100: Ctrl + Z

Lastly, Ctrl + Z serve as the shortcut for the Undo function. This will reverse your latest command in Excel.

And that finishes our countdown for the Top 100 keyboard shortcuts in Microsoft Excel. To wrap things up, the last chapter will provide some pointers in "memorizing" these shortcuts the easiest way.

Chapter 6: Pointers for the Excel Novice

Most people will most likely feel daunted with the mere volume of shortcuts in this book. "How can I ever memorize a hundred of these combinations?", says most people. This fear of memorization only impedes the learning process. As such, you should stay away from this negative thinking.

Practice a Couple of Shortcuts Every Week

To be able to remember these shortcuts effectively, you should use them as often as you could. Have this book by your side always so that you will have a guide as you try to absorb each of these shortcuts. Better yet, you can jot down a couple of shortcuts in a small list so that you can try some of these tricks in your school or the office.

After finishing let's say at least five shortcuts for a week, add another five in the succeeding weeks. Just don't forget the previous shortcuts that you have learned. In no time, you will be able to use these keyboard combinations without the help of a cheat sheet.

Don't Use the Numeric Keypad

Although most people on the go use laptops such as students, many people still use the full-sized keyboard that has a built-in numeric keypad at the right side.

Although several characters in the listed shortcuts are there, the Microsoft Excel does not recognize the use of numeric keypad in its shortcuts. As such, you shouldn't try to practice these shortcuts via the numeric keypad; just use the main keyboard itself.

That ends all the pointers in this guide for Excel shortcuts. With that, you should apply all the learnings that you have discovered through this book in your daily Excel tasks. Hopefully, you'll be a more efficient Excel user as you incorporate these shortcuts in using the said spreadsheet program.

Conclusion

Thank you again for purchasing this book!

I hope this book was able to help you to learn the secrets behind mastering Microsoft Excel, which are the 100 keyboard shortcuts.

The next step is to make use of these shortcuts every time you operate on the Excel application. Through this, you can now easily work on your Excel spreadsheets with only a minimal use of a mouse.

Finally, if you enjoyed this book, please take the time to share your thoughts and post a review on Amazon. We do our best to reach out to readers and provide the best value we can. Your positive review will help us achieve that. It'd be greatly appreciated!

Thank you and good luck!

Check Out My Other Books

Below you'll find some of my other popular books that are popular on Amazon and Kindle as well. Simply click on the links below to check them out. Alternatively, you can visit my author page on Amazon to see other work done by me.

C Programming Success in a Day

Android Programming in a Day

C ++ Programming Success in a Day

Python Programming in a Day

PHP Programming Professional Made Easy

HTML Professional Programming Made Easy

JavaScript Programming Made Easy

CSS Programming Professional Made Easy

Windows 8 Tips for Beginners

If the links do not work, for whatever reason, you can simply search for these titles on the Amazon website to find them.

www.ingramcontent.com/pod-product-compliance
Lightning Source LLC
Chambersburg PA
CBHW061044050326
40689CB00012B/2968
9781511949965